The Alphabet Book

Story by Monique Dorcely

https://pathtogrowllc.com/

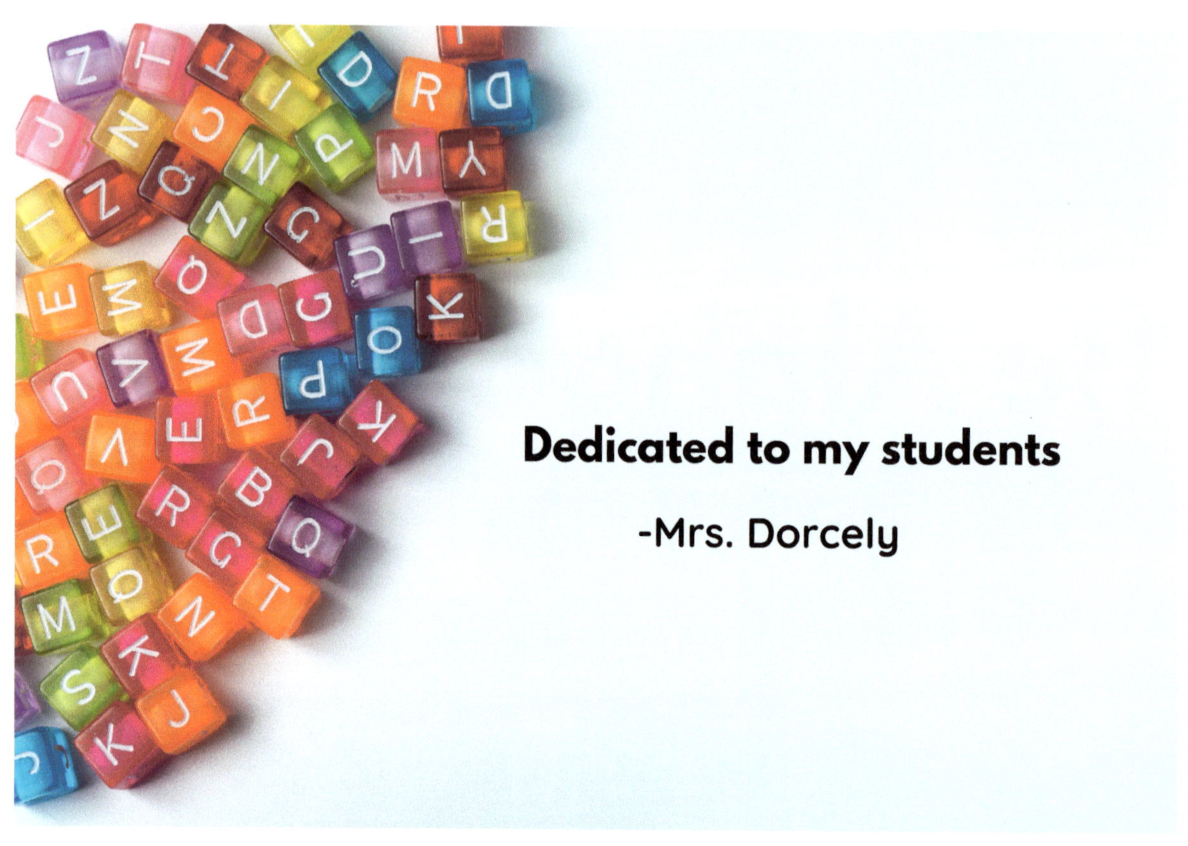

Dedicated to my students

-Mrs. Dorcely

This book belongs to:

____

Ms. Pat brings toys and letters for the letter investigation games.

Ms. Pat says, "Today is
Letters and Objects Investigation Day."
What letters do these objects begin with?

What object begins with the letter a?

A is for apple.

Bb

What object begins with the letter b?

B is for ball.

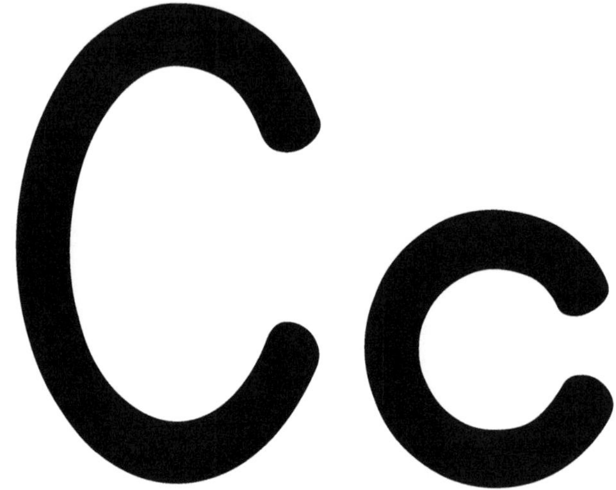

What object begins with the letter c?

C is for car.

What object begins with the letter d?

D is for duck.

What object begins with the letter e?

E is for egg.

Ff

What object begins with the letter f?

F is for fish.

What object begins with the letter g?

G is for goat.

What object begins with the letter h?

H is for hammer.

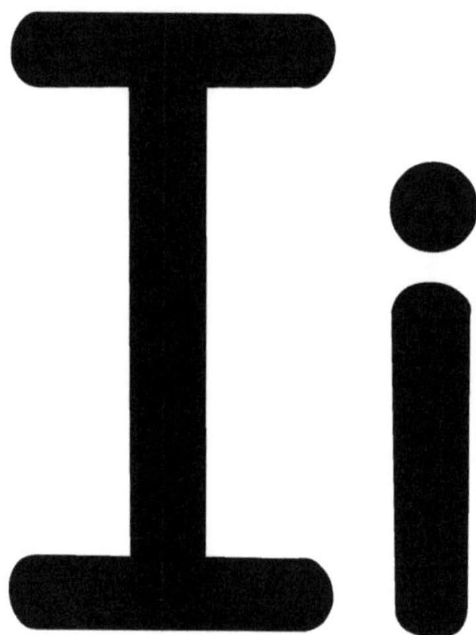

What object begins with the letter i?

I is for igloo.

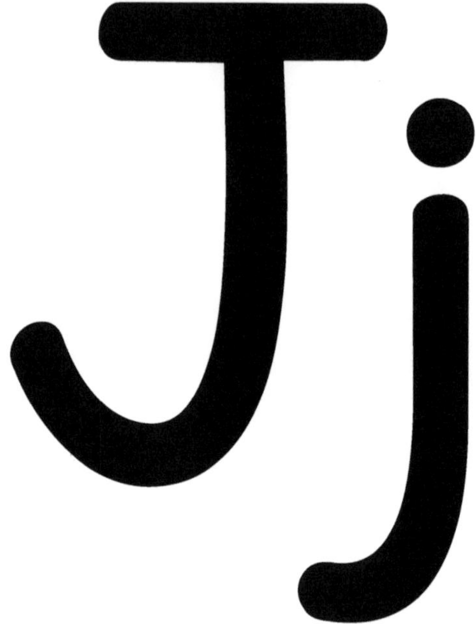

What object begins with the letter j?

J is for jar.

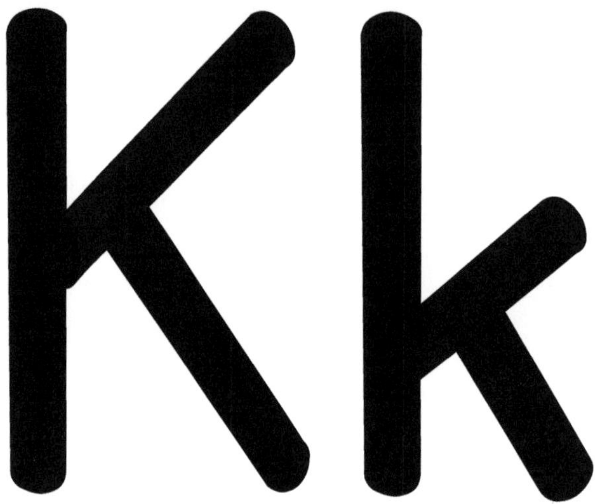

What object begins with the letter k?

K is for key.

What object begins with the letter l?

L is for lion.

What object begins with the letter m?

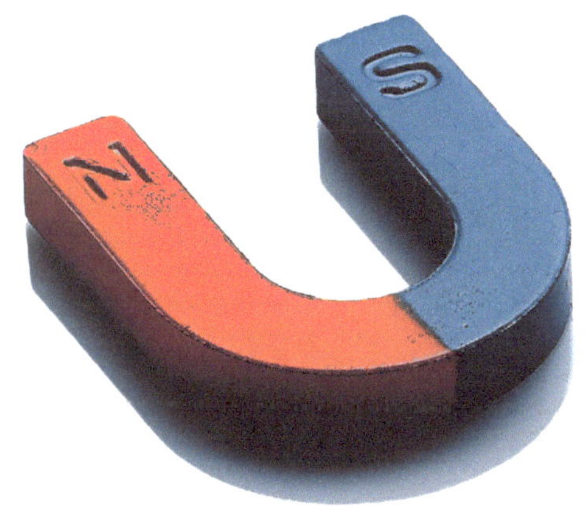

M is for magnet.

What object begins with the letter n?

N is for net.

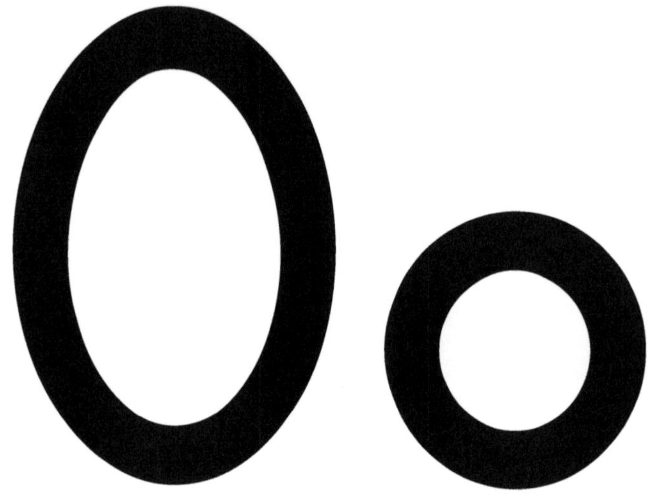

What object begins with the letter o?

O is for orange.

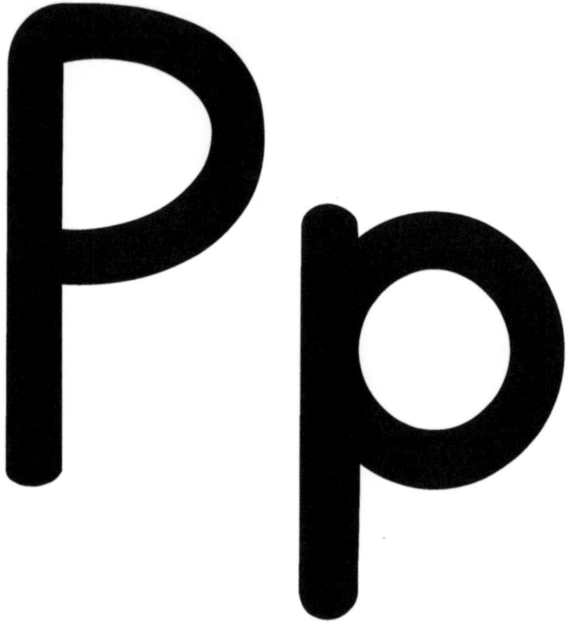

What object begins with the letter p?

P is for pot.

What object begins with the letter q?

Q is for queen.

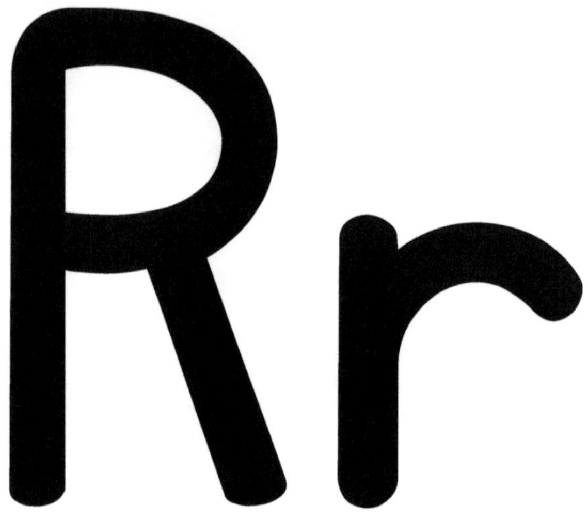

What object begins with the letter r?

R is for rake.

Ss

What object begins with the letter s?

S is for sandal.

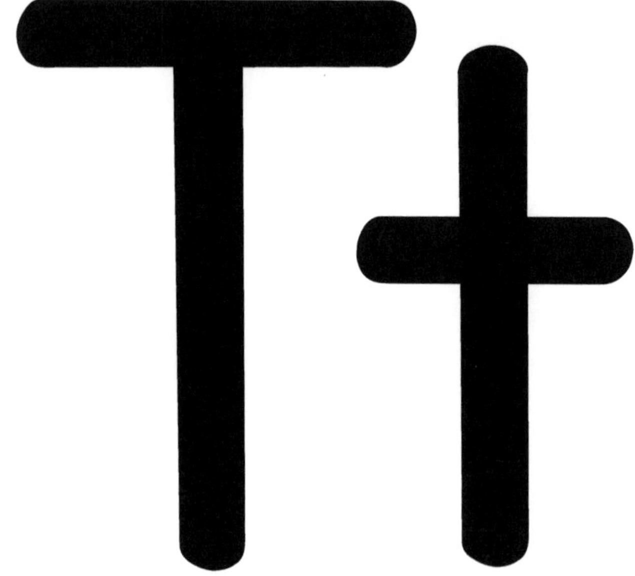

What object begins with the letter t?

T is for turtle.

What object begins with the letter u?

U is for umbrella.

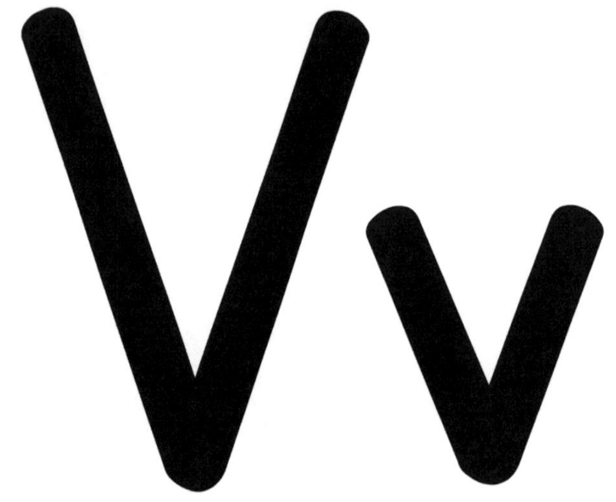

What object begins with the letter v?

V is for vase.

What object begins with the letter w?

W is for watch.

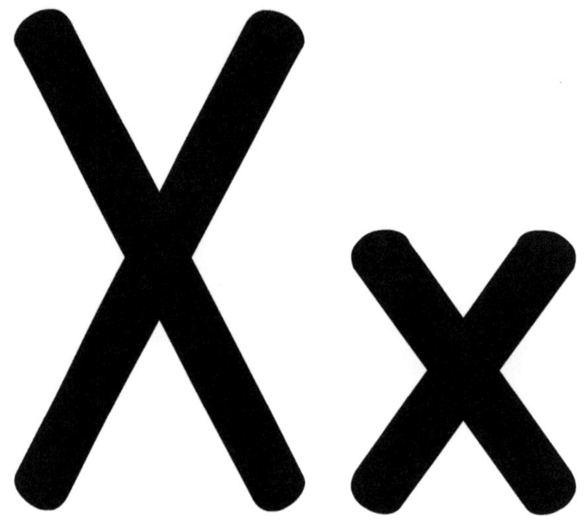

What object begins with the letter x?

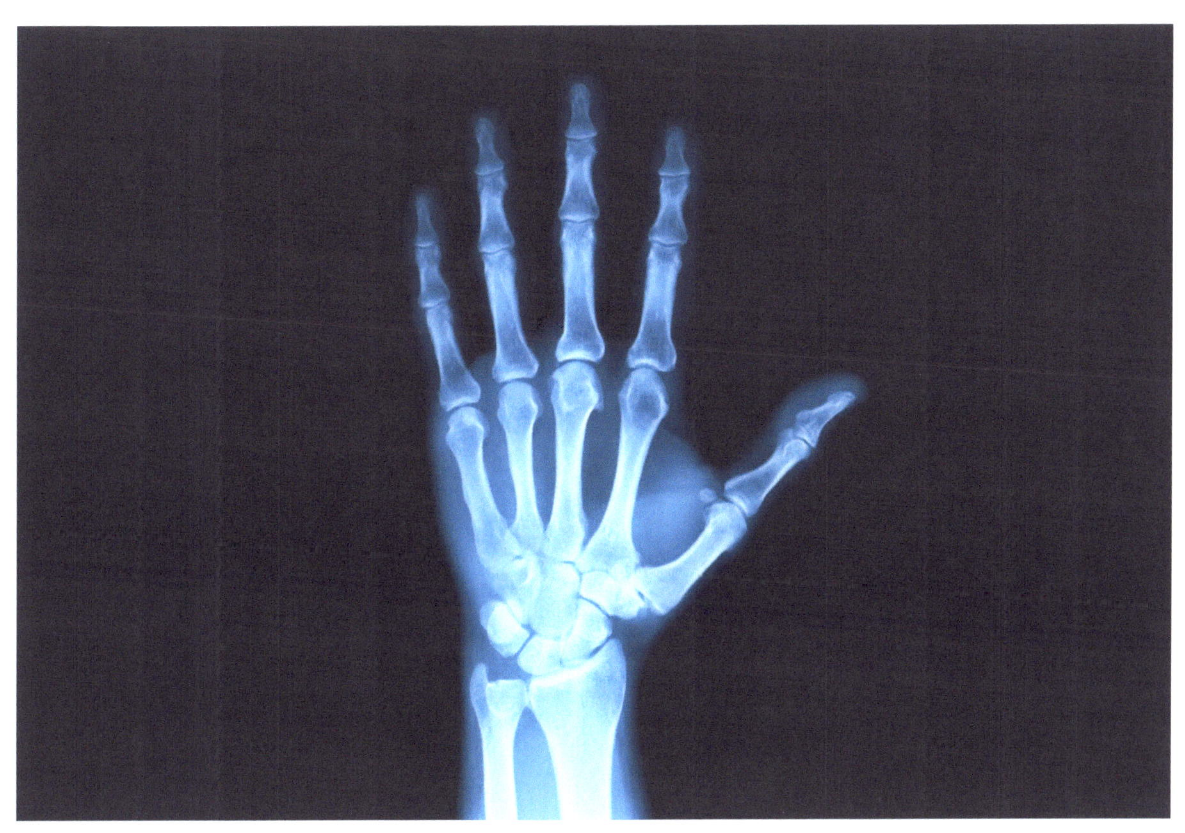

X is for X-ray.

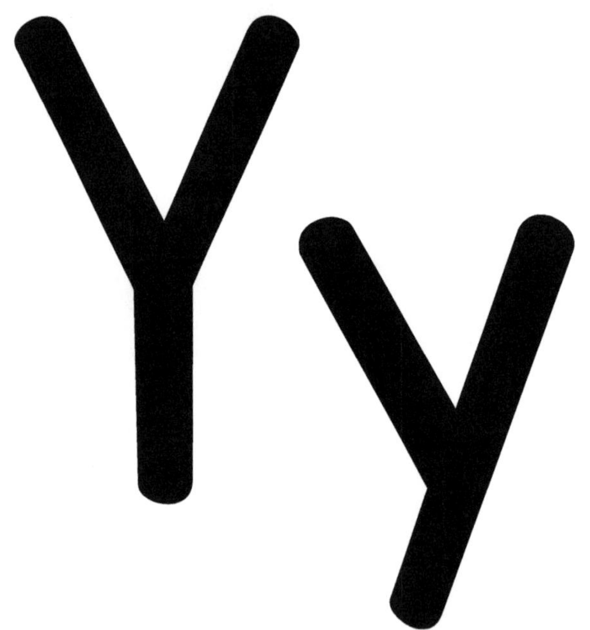

What object begins with the letter y?

Y is for yoyo.

Zz

What object begins with the letter z?

Z is for Zebra.

After the children play, "The Letters and Objects Investigation Game," the children make and eat alphabet soup.

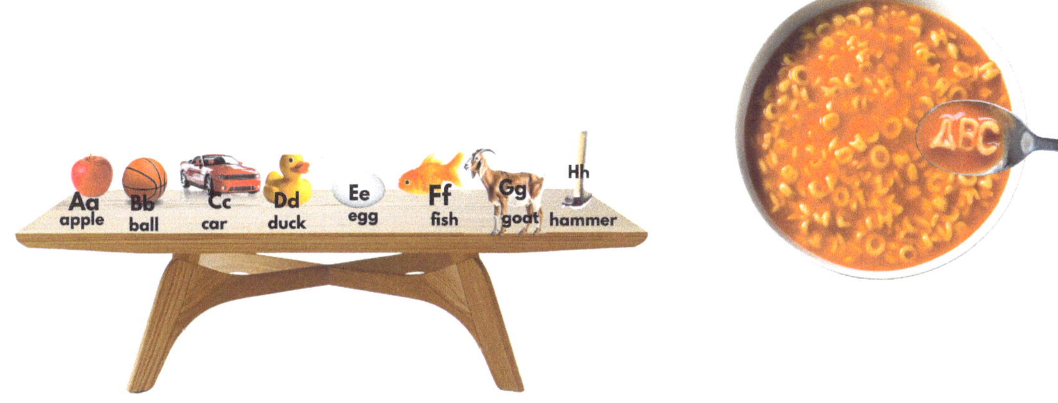

Now it is your turn to play the objects and letters game, and eat the alphabet soup.

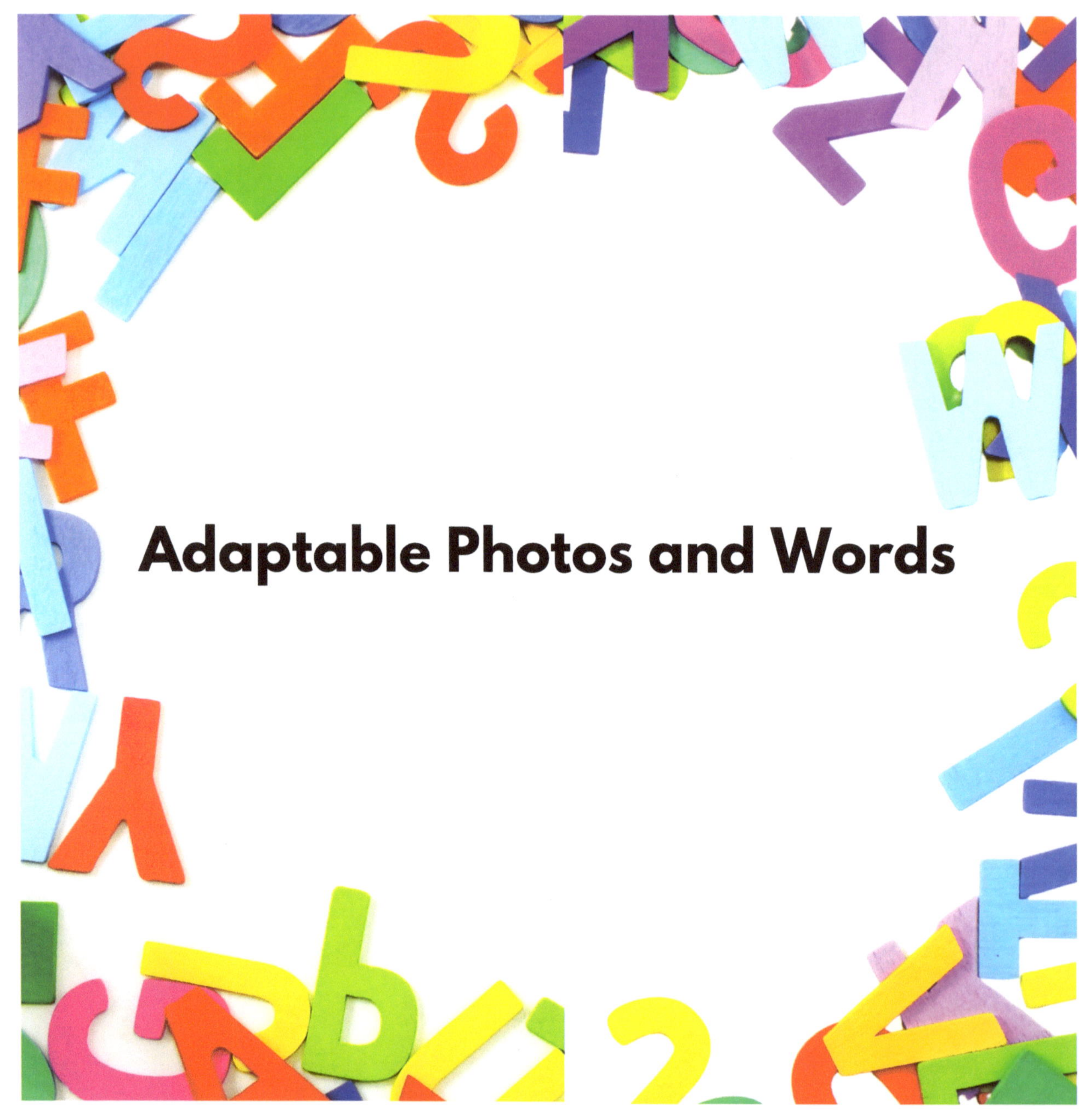

Adaptable Photos and Words

	THE ALPHABET BOOK ABC GAMES! 	THE ALPHABET BOOK ABC GAMES!
	toys and letters 	toys and letters
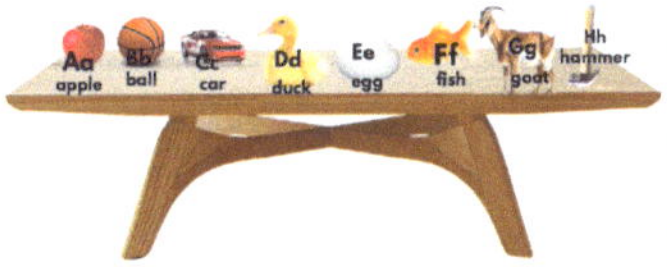	letters and objects 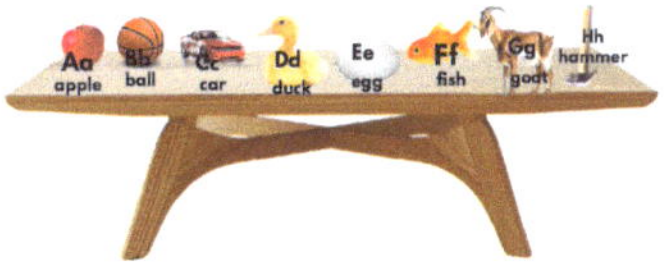	letters and objects
	alphabet soup 	alphabet soup

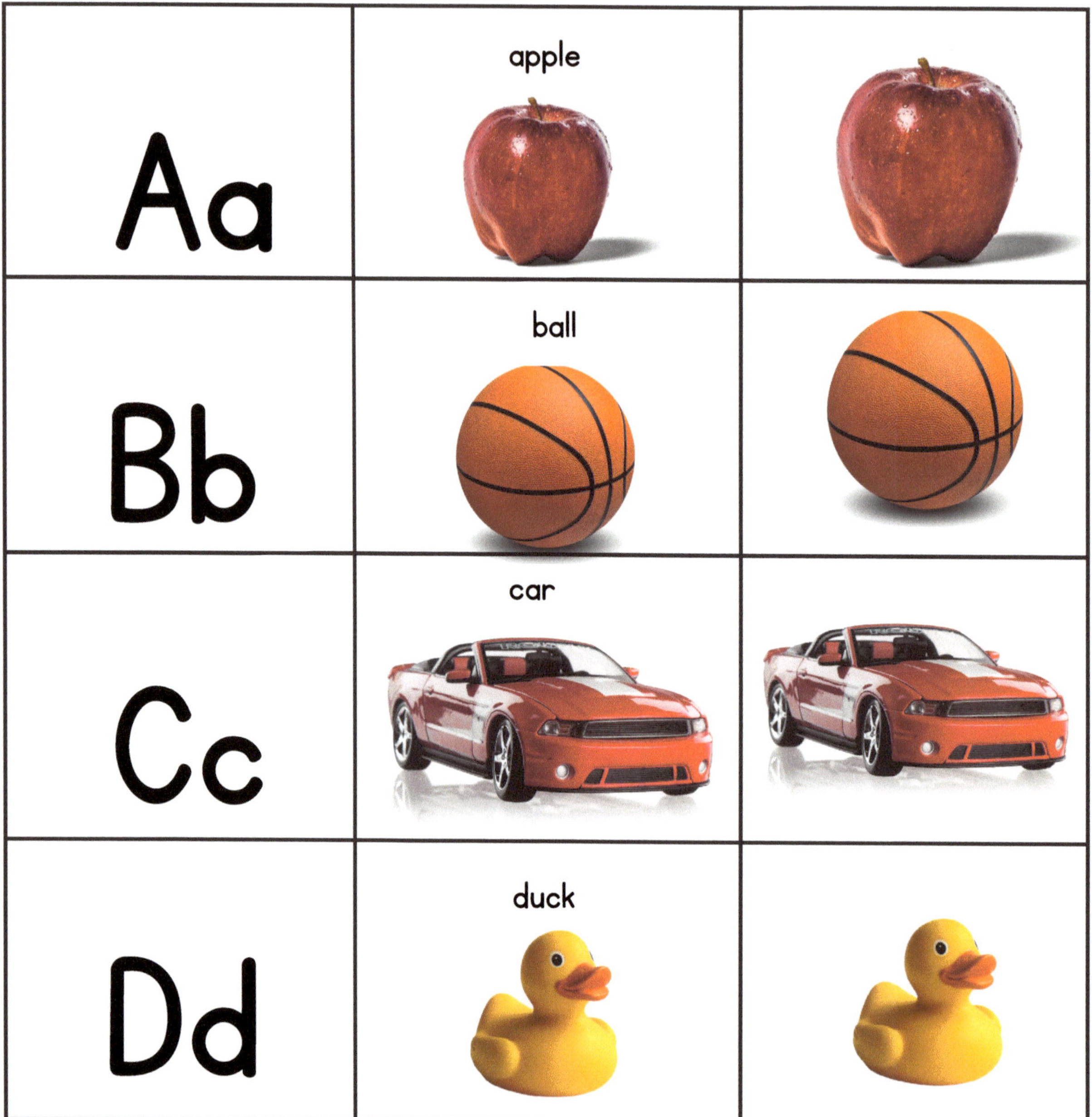
Aa
apple
Bb
ball
Cc
car
Dd
duck

Ee	egg	
Ff	fish 	
Gg	goat 	
Hh	hammer 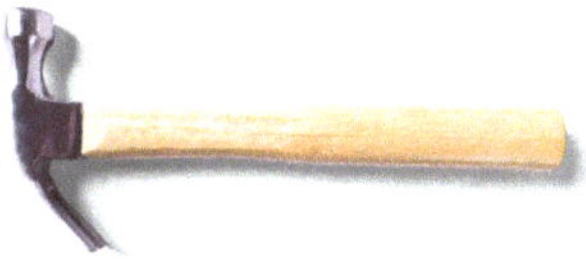	

Ii	igloo 	
Jj	jar	
Kk	key 	
Ll	lion 	

Mm	magnet 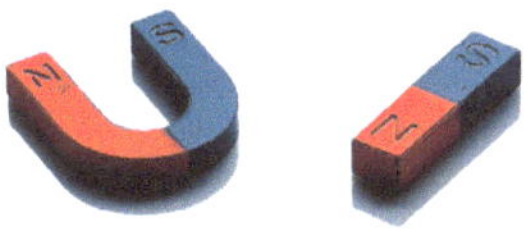	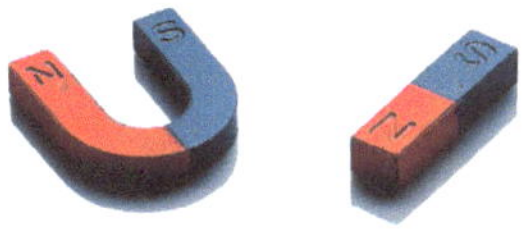
Nn	net 	
Oo	orange 	
Pp	pot 	

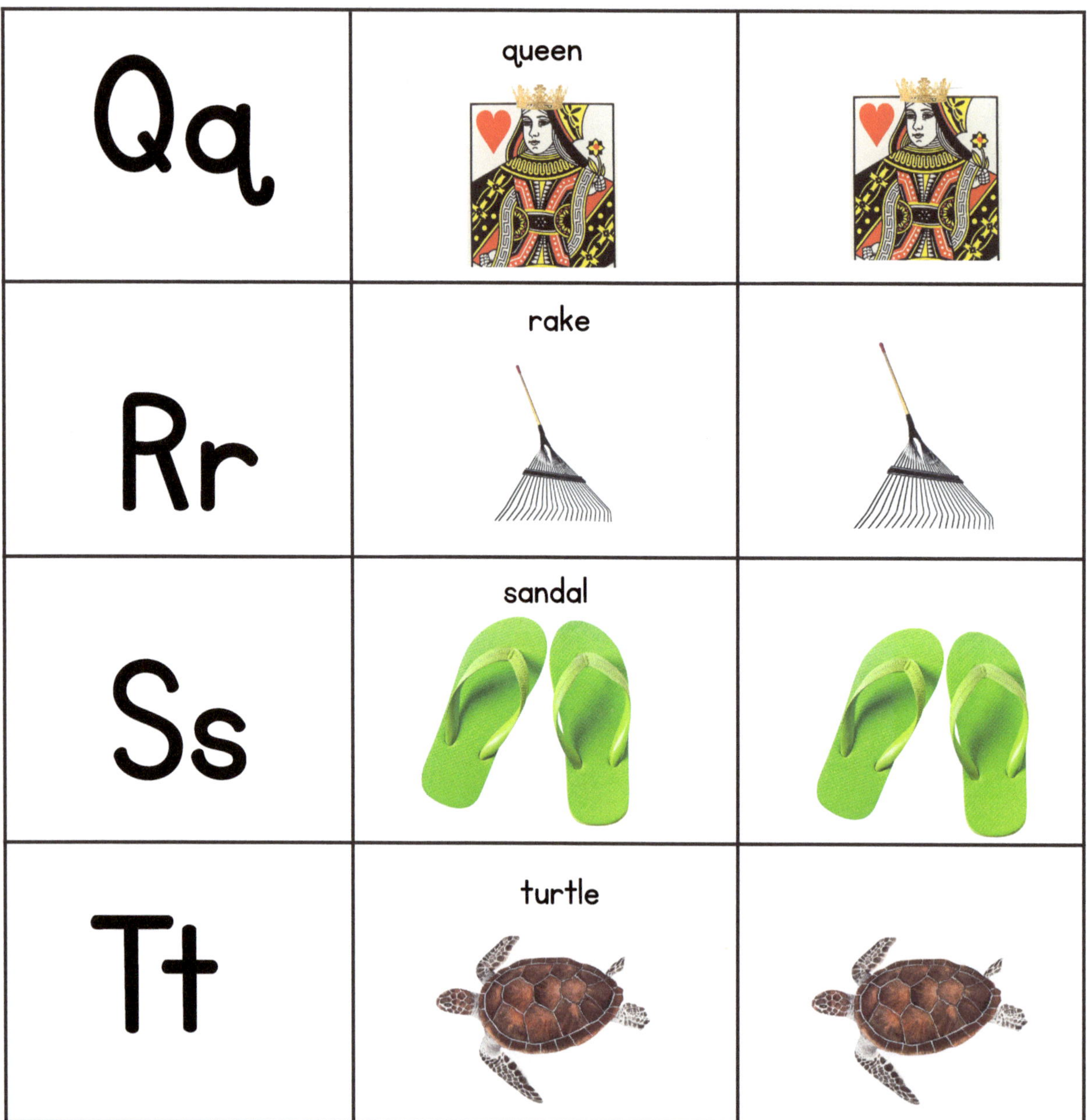
Qq
queen
Rr
rake
Ss
sandal
Tt
turtle

Uu	umbrella 	
Vv	vase	
Ww	watch 	
Xx	X-ray 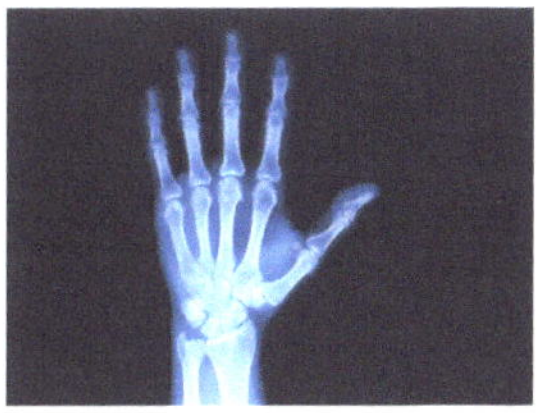	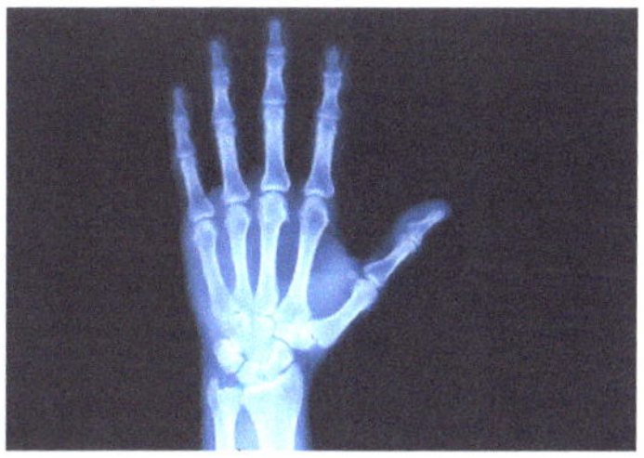

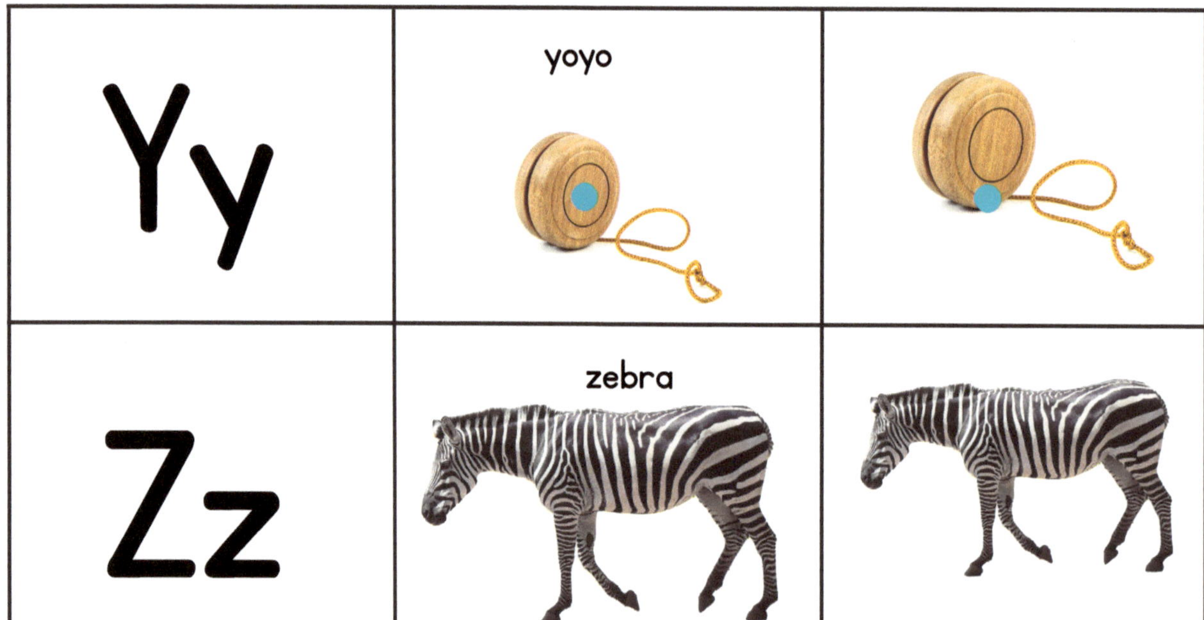
Yy
yoyo
Zz
zebra

Aa	apple 	apple
Bb	ball 	ball
Cc	car 	car
Dd	duck 	duck

Ee	egg	egg
Ff	fish 	fish
Gg	goat 	goat
Hh	hammer 	hammer

Ii	igloo 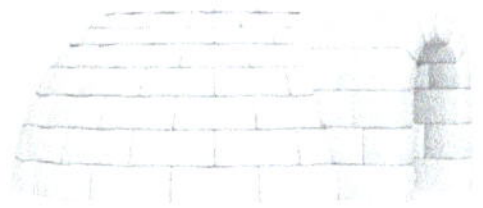	igloo
Jj	jar	jar
Kk	key 	key
Ll	lion 	lion

Mm	magnet	magnet
Nn	net	net
Oo	orange	orange
Pp	pot	pot

Qq	queen 	queen
Rr	rake 	rake
Ss	sandal 	sandal
Tt	turtle 	turtle

Uu	umbrella 	umbrella
Vv	vase	vase
Ww	watch 	watch
Xx	X-ray 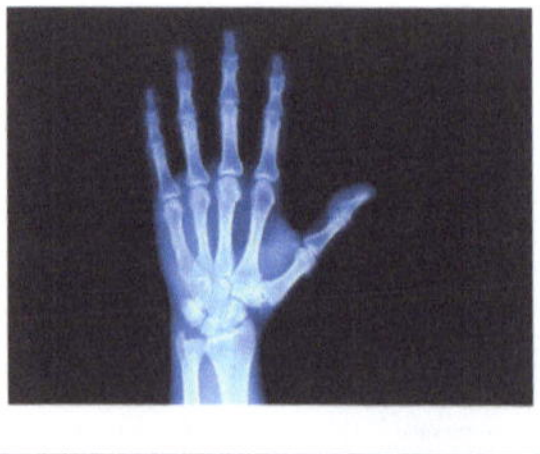	X-ray

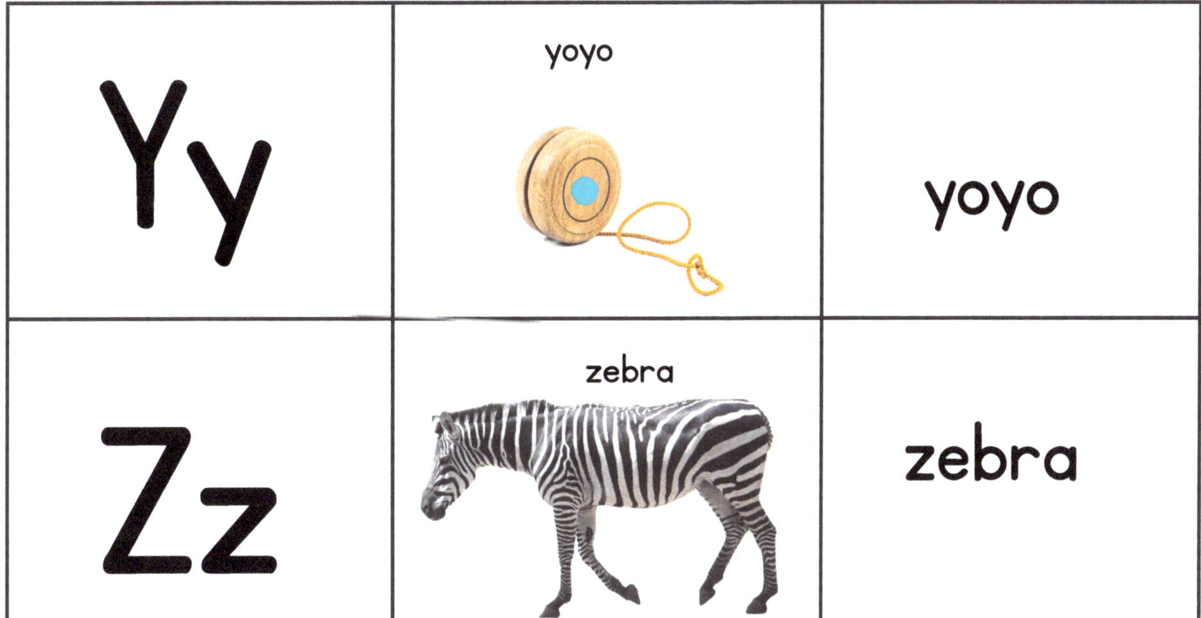
Yy
yoyo
yoyo
Zz
zebra
zebra

www.ingramcontent.com/pod-product-compliance
Lightning Source LLC
LaVergne TN
LVHW070142110826
845147LV00002B/307

* 9 7 9 8 9 9 3 3 1 4 7 5 4 *